TENNIS
RULES AND TECHNIQUES IN
PICTURES

MICHAEL J. BROWN

A PERIGEE BOOK

Perigee Books
are published by
The Putnam Publishing Group
200 Madison Avenue
New York, NY 10016

Library of Congress Cataloging-in-Publication Data

Brown, Michael, date.
   Tennis rules and techniques in pictures.

   1. Tennis. 2. Tennis—Rules. I. Title.
GV995.B6929   1987   796.342'2   87-2416
ISBN 0-399-51405-8

Printed in the United States of America
   3 4 5 6 7 8 9 10

CONTENTS

INTRODUCTION

Once solely the pastime of aristocrats and royalty, tennis has become one of the most popular games in the world. In the last thirty years participation has soared; today millions of people around the globe play the game. That's not hard to believe when you consider that tennis has been evolving for hundreds of years. In fact, the roots of modern tennis stretch back to ancient Egypt. Archeological evidence indicates that stick-and-ball games were being played in that part of the world as early as 4000 B.C. During the Middle Ages, invading armies from the Middle East brought to Europe a game of handball that was an ancestor of tennis. Europeans developed their own variations, which in turn were carried back east with the crusaders.

By the dawn of the Renaissance, this game was firmly entrenched in Northern Europe, where it was played primarily by royalty, courtiers, and ecclesiastics. These players were not noted for having callused hands, so to protect themselves they first wrapped their hands, then wore gloves. Eventually the players hit the ball with boards instead of with their hands. These crude paddles gained popularity and were modified; by the fifteenth century, players were employing rackets that vaguely resembled the ones we use today. There was, however, no regulation court. The game was played indoors or out, in moats or cloisters, and physical surroundings were considered natural hazards.

A game very similar to today's tennis evolved in Britain during the 1860s and 1870s. Its most well-known proponent was Major Walter C. Wingfield, who called his amalgam of various other popular court games "Sphairistike." It was introduced in the U.S. by Mary Ewing Outerbridge in 1874.

As the game spread along the East Coast of the U.S., tennis clubs were formed. At the same time the game's popularity continued to grow in England, where the All England Croquet and Tennis Club held its first tournament in 1877. The rules laid down for this tournament were adopted by the assembled U.S. tennis clubs at their 1881 conclave. Soon tennis spread to all corners of the world. In the United States today tennis courts are found everywhere, from apartment complexes to city parks to the tops of high-rise buildings.

Countless national and regional organizations, such as the United States Tennis Association (USTA) and the Lawn Tennis Association (LTA) in Britain, exist worldwide. In addition to these, international organizations including the International Lawn Tennis Federation (ILTF, the nominal controlling body of the game), World Championship Tennis, Inc. (WCT), and the Association of Tennis Professionals (ATP) help to advance tennis all over the world. Major tournaments such as the U.S., French, and Australian opens, the Davis Cup, and the queen of all tournaments, Wimbledon, are promoted and broadcast throughout the world.

Credit for the stupendous popularity of tennis cannot, however, be claimed by any one organization or event, but by the game itself. Not only does it develop players' stamina, strength, and agility, but their skill and intelligence as well. It is a game played by all ages, and unlike other sports, it need not be given up as one grows older. One advantage of tennis is that it is played with a minimum of equipment. It is also easier for a tennis player to find a partner than to round up the number of players that many other sports require. Great matches can be played between opponents of widely varying physical types and styles of play. Tennis has one other advantage: it can be played equally well by both sexes.

It is not unusual for people who first meet as opponents on the tennis court to go on to become good friends. One of the reasons that tennis is a great way to meet people is that the scoring and "calling" of the tennis match is a cooperative effort. Usually, players call the games themselves, each player calling his own half of the court and his opponent's foot faults. Because of this, it is only fair to your opponent and to yourself to have a precise knowledge of the rules of the game.

Before sitting down with the rule book, however, you should be aware of one very important reason that fiercely competitive opponents can call their own game, have a satisfying match, and walk off the court as friends. This is the Code.

The Code is basically a set of informal laws of tennis. For more than a century and up until the last few years, players have almost universally adhered to this tennis tradition. The spirit of the Code is fair play, honorable and polite behavior, and a minimum of "gamesmanship." It was formalized by Colonel Nick Powel in 1974. To paraphrase him:

- Always give your opponent the benefit of the doubt; if you are not absolutely sure a ball is out, presume that it is good.
- It's a player's responsibility to call all balls on his side, to help make calls on the opponent's side if asked, and to call out any of his own balls that he clearly sees go out on his opponent's side.
- If you catch a ball that is in play you lose the point, even if you are outside the court.
- In doubles, when partners disagree about whether a ball is out, the ball must be considered good.
- The partner of the player who is receiving service should call the service line. The receiver himself calls the center and side lines.
- It is rude to return a service that is obviously out; it is unsportsmanlike if you know this bothers the server.
- When returning a stray ball to another court, hit it so that it goes to the server or another player on the first bounce.
- Dress neatly. When visiting a club for the first time, you cannot err if you dress all in white.
- Each player should provide five minutes of warm-up, hitting his shots directly to his opponents. Don't confuse warm-up with practice.
- To prevent arguments about the score, the server should announce

the set score before his first serve and the game score before each point.

Don't fool yourself into thinking that the Code is optional. The vast majority of players follow the Code even if they have never seen it in writing. Unless you are John McEnroe, you may find that breaches of tennis etiquette will make it difficult to find a partner.

PART I: THE GAME

EQUIPMENT

The Court

The singles court is a 78-foot-long, 27-foot-wide rectangle. The court for doubles is the same length as the singles court, but "alleys" are added to increase the width of the court by 4½ feet on each side. Most of the lines bounding the court are one to two inches thick, although the center

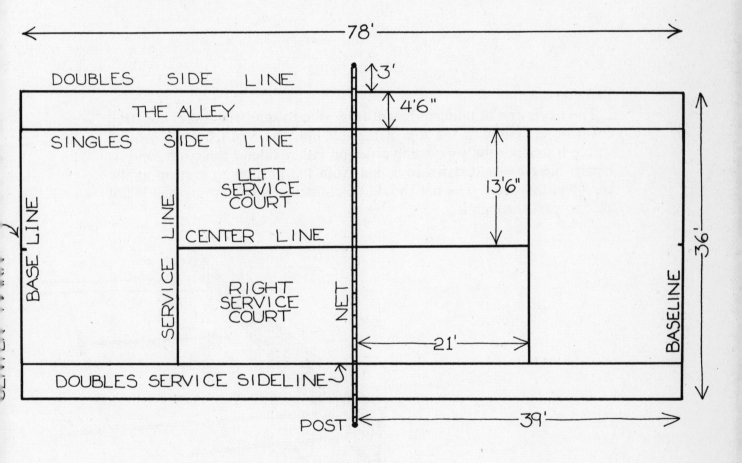

The court.

service line must be at least two inches and the baseline may be up to four inches thick, to make it easy to see from the opposite side. All these lines are part of the areas they describe. This means that if a ball hits the line during play, it is in bounds and still playable.

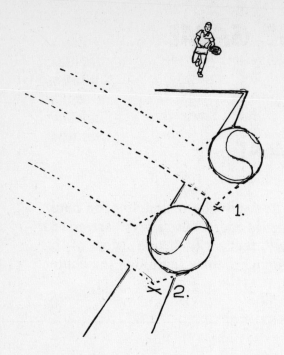

Ball number 1 is out, ball number 2 is in.

The Net

The net is one of uniform height from side to side. However, the strap covering the cable at the top of the net must be 3'6" from the ground where it touches the supporting poles on either side of the court, and its height must be held down to 3 feet from the ground by a strap at the center of the court. The net should be constructed so that the ball is not able to pass through it.

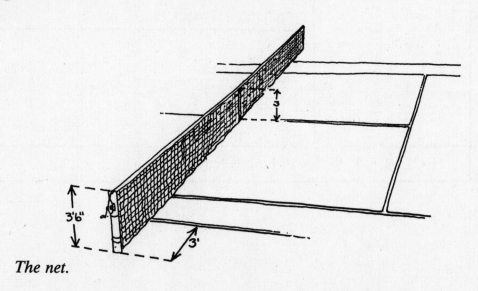

The net.

The posts supporting the net should be 3 feet outside the court. If a doubles court is used for singles, the net should be supported to the proper height of 3'6" by singles sticks, which should be placed 3 feet outside the singles court.

10

The Ball

The ball should be approximately 2½ inches in diameter, weigh 2 ounces, and be either white or yellow. If it has seams they should be stitchless. A tennis ball should be responsive but not too lively. A good informal test is to hold the ball high over the head and let it fall onto a cement court. It should bound back to approximately armpit height. Officially, the ball should bounce more than 53 inches and less than 58 inches when dropped from 100 inches upon a concrete base.

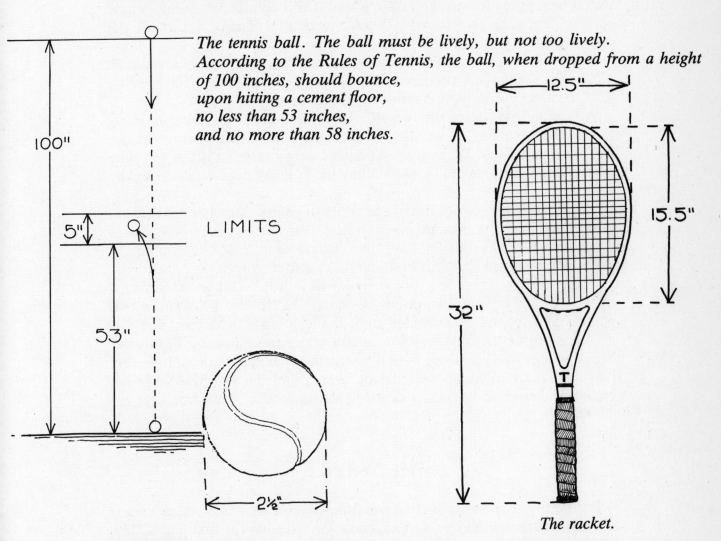

The tennis ball. The ball must be lively, but not too lively. According to the Rules of Tennis, the ball, when dropped from a height of 100 inches, should bounce, upon hitting a cement floor, no less than 53 inches, and no more than 58 inches.

The racket.

The Racket

The hitting surface of the racket should be flat and uniform, with one set of regularly interlaced or banded strings. Strings should not be less dense in the center or "sweet spot" than in any other part of the racket. The racket should be no more than 32 inches in overall length, and the hitting surface should be no more than 12½ inches in width, including the frame. Exclusive of the frame, the strung surface, even with today's oversize rackets, should not exceed 15½ inches in length or 11½ inches in width. The balance or shape of the racket may not be adjusted during play.

PLAYING THE GAME

The rudiments of tennis are not difficult to grasp. A tennis match is made up of a series of "rallies." A rally occurs when two (or four in doubles) people stand on opposite sides of the net and hit the ball back and forth with their rackets. Each player tries to hit the ball either before it bounces (this is called a volley) or after it has bounced once. Each player also tries to hit the ball so that it lands in his opponent's court, and if he's trying to win, he hits it where it will be difficult or impossible for his opponent to return it. When the opponent can't return it, the player gains a point.

Each rally starts with the service. Players alternate service after each game; the server gets two chances to make a good serve. Each time he fails to do so properly, it is either a "fault" or a "let."

A fault means one of the two chances is used up. If both are used up, the point will be lost. A let means the chance will be taken over—it does not count as a fault. When a player is receiving a serve, it is the one time when he may not volley; he must allow the ball to bounce once after the serve.

Tennis matches are not timed like football games. Matches are divided into games and sets. The player who first wins four or more points wins a "game." (Games must be won by a margin of at least two points; the game will be extended until that margin is achieved.)

The player who first wins six games wins a "set." Just as games must be won by a margin of two points, sets must be won by a margin of two games. The set will be extended until that margin is achieved. There is an attending tie-break system for certain major tournaments. In this tie-break system, if a set is tied 6–6, a tie-break game is played, and the first player to reach 7 points wins the tie-break, and the set. The tie-break system is described in greater detail in the appendix of this book (pages 79–80).

THE SERVICE

Before the players begin the game, they decide by a toss which end of the court each will occupy and who will serve during the first game. The player winning the toss may choose whether or not to serve *or* choose an end of the court; or he may have his opponent make one of these choices. In any event, one player has the pick of the service and the other the pick of court ends.

The service starts play. The server stands on one side of the net and the receiver on the other. The server must have both feet at rest behind the baseline and inside the imaginary continuations of the center mark and the sideline (this means the doubles sideline during doubles play, or the singles sideline when playing singles).

Although the server's position and stance are highly regulated, receivers

The server is in position ready to serve.

CENTER MARK

The receiver may stand where he likes.

may stand wherever they like, as long as they are on their own side of the net.

The foot fault is a very common error in the service. This fault is committed if, between taking a "ready to serve" stance and striking the ball, the server

- changes position by walking or running;
- or steps on the baseline or the imaginary extension of the sideline or center mark.

The server is committing a foot fault with each foot.

If a fault is called, the service is not good. Again, if the server commits two faults, the point is lost.

The server should not put the ball into play unless the receiver is ready. Once the receiver has indicated that he is ready, he may not, under normal circumstances, become unready. Also, if the receiver makes any attempt to return the ball, it indicates that he was ready.

The receiver was not ready.

After indicating that she is ready, the receiver may not generally become unready.

The first point is always started from the right service court, the second from the left, and so on. After each point is played, the server alternates sides. If a player becomes confused and mistakenly plays a portion of a match while serving from the wrong side of the court, all subsequent play, points, faults, etc. shall stand. However, the server's position should be corrected as soon as the error is discovered.

The server must toss the ball in the air with his free hand and must strike it before it hits the ground. It must be sent over the net and bounce in the service court diagonally opposite before it may be returned. The service is a fault if:

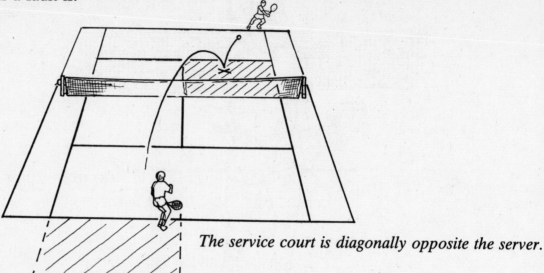

The service court is diagonally opposite the server.

- the server commits a foot fault;
- the server fails to serve into the proper service court;
- the server serves from the wrong side of the court and it is immediately noticed;
- the server misses the ball while attempting to strike it;
- the served ball first strikes a permanent fixture (such as the net support poles, the singles sticks, or the doubles portion of the net if singles is being played).

The server has missed the ball— this is a service fault.

It is not a service fault if the server:

- moves his feet slightly due to the service motion;
- accidentally throws up two balls during the service toss;
- does not swing at a tossed ball;
- serves "underhand";
- serves to a receiver who is not ready and misses the correct service court.

If the first service is a fault, the server serves a second service from the same court. A fault on the second service means the loss of the point.

If the server does not swing, this will not be a service fault.

Service Lets

If a service let is called when the server has already made one service fault, only the let service is retaken, not both serves.

It is a service let if the ball hits the net but continues forward and falls into the proper service court.

The ball has hit the top of the net and bounced into the proper service court. This is a service let.

It is a service let if the ball is served when the receiver is not ready.

It is a service let if the served ball glances off the net and hits an opponent before touching the ground.

It is important to remember that a let serve does not annul a prior service fault.

This is a service let.

Other Lets

Unlike a service let, if a let is called during play for any other reason, then the whole point is replayed, not just that service. Some reasons to replay the point are:

- the ball becomes defective;
- there is an erroneous call by an official;
- a ball bounces in from another court and interferes with play;
- any interference occurs;
- the receiver causes an excessive service delay.

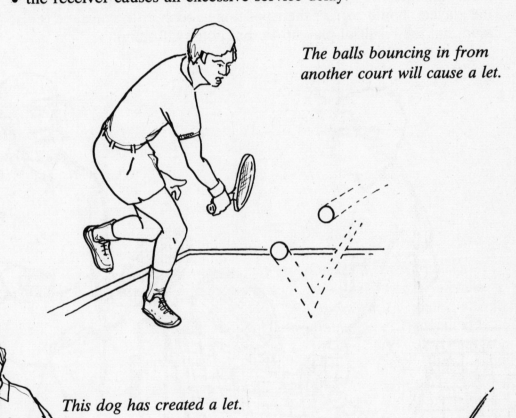

The balls bouncing in from another court will cause a let.

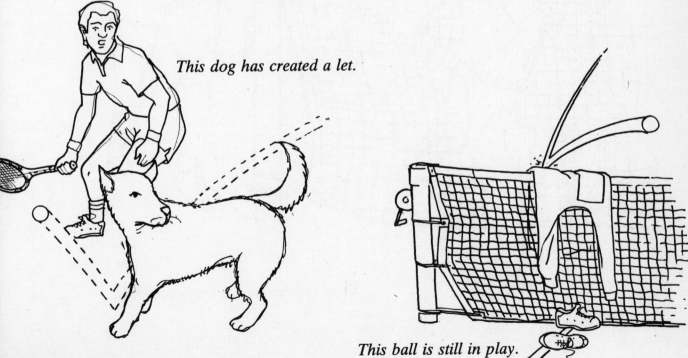

This dog has created a let.

This ball is still in play.

A let should not be claimed if both players agree to start play under a given set of conditions; for example, with a pair of sweats hanging on the net. When the ball hits them, it remains in play.

At the end of the first game, the server and receiver exchange roles, and they continue to alternate serving and receiving each game for the entire match.

The players must also change ends of the court. They do this at the end of the first, third, and every subsequent alternate game in each set. If the total number of games is even when the set ends, the change is not made until the end of the first game of the next set. If a mistake is made, the players should correct their position as soon as the mistake is discovered, but the result of play up to that point will stand.

These opponents are changing ends.

WINNING AND LOSING POINTS

The Ball in Play

The ball is in play from the time it is delivered in service; unless fault or let is called, it remains in play until the point is decided. Even shots which are obviously going out are considered to be in play until they actually land out. Volleying or catching them before they strike the ground results in loss of the point.

"The ball is in play from the time it is delivered in service."

This player loses the point even though the ball was obviously going to land out.

Similarly, let's say that during an exciting rally a player only manages to get the ball over the net after two bounces. However, neither player is sure how many bounces the ball took, so the play continues. In this case, the ball is considered to be in play and the point cannot be claimed later.

This ball was obviously going out,
but the player hit it and therefore loses the point.

If the play continues, a point cannot be claimed later.

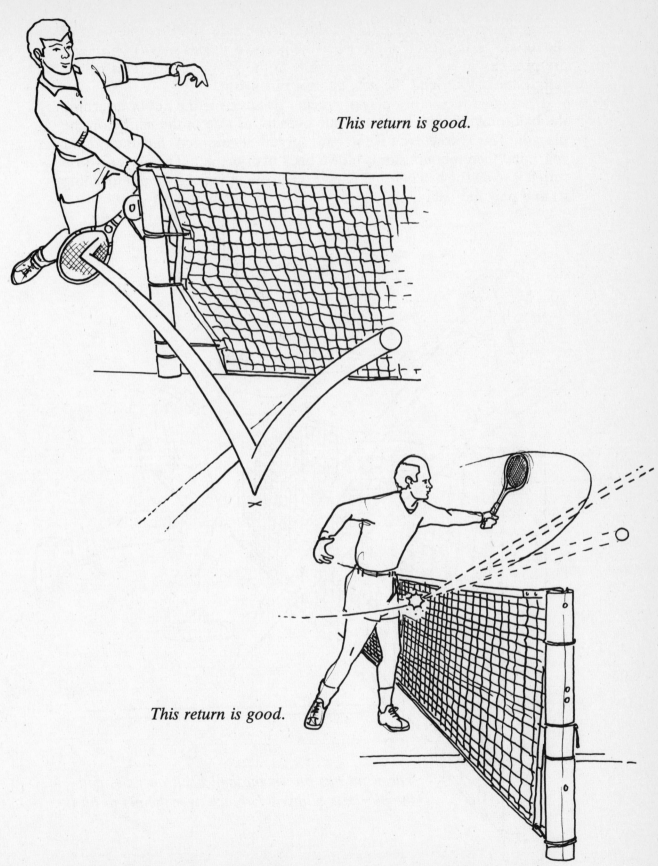

This return is good.

This return is good.

It is a good return and the rally continues if the ball, before bouncing twice, is played back over the net.

It is a good return if the ball is returned outside or below the level of the top of the net, even if it touches the posts or singles sticks (whichever are properly in use) as long as it lands in the proper court. This means hitting the ball around the net, but not through it.

It is a good return if a player's racket passes over the net in returning the ball, provided the ball has come over to his side of the net before he plays it. This is true even if the ball, served or returned, hits the proper court and then rebounds or is blown back over the net. The player whose turn it is to hit the ball has the right to reach over the net (without touching it) and play the ball.

The wind has blown the ball back over the net; the player is allowed to reach over the net to hit it.

The extra ball was on the court when the point was begun, so play continues.

It is a good return if a player successfully hits a ball that strikes another ball lying on the court.

The rule book and common sense dictate that the ball is out of play if it lodges in the net. But unlike the service, it remains in play if during a rally it hits the net, cords, straps, posts, or sticks, as long as it passes them

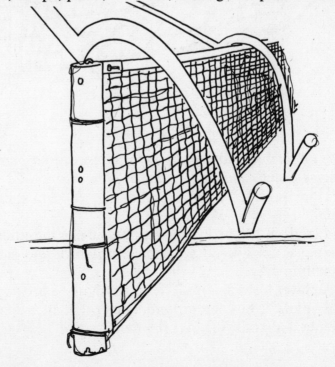

Either of these balls would remain in play during a rally.

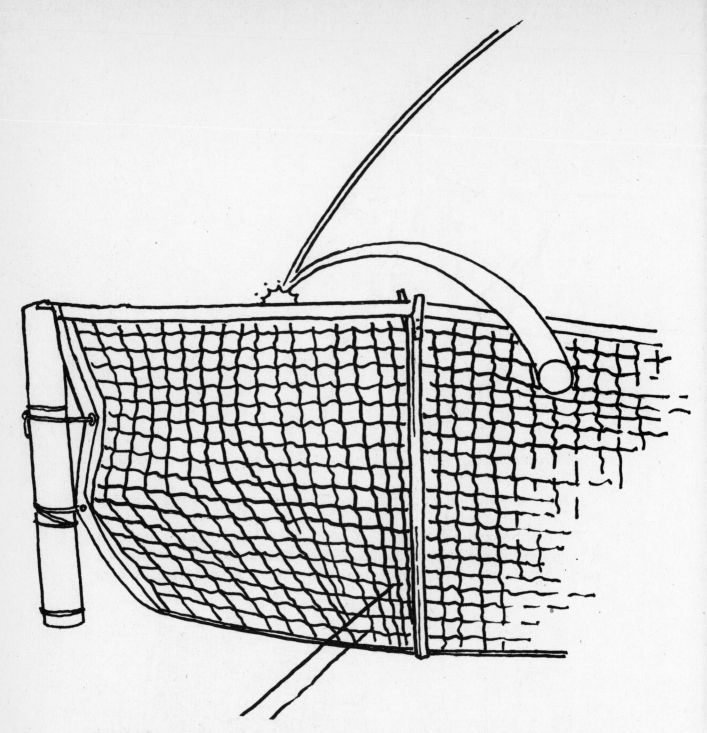

The doubles portion of the net is considered a permanent fixture during a singles match. This ball is not in play.

and lands in the proper court. (In singles the unused doubles portion of the net is considered a permanent fixture and a ball hitting it does not remain in play.)

A player loses a point if he or anything he is carrying touches the served ball before it hits the ground. This prevents a receiver from standing at the net and volleying an opponent's serve.

*An illegal return on a service
and a point for the server.*

This player loses the point.

The point is lost by the player hitting the ball out.

A player loses a point if he fails to return the ball before it bounces twice.

A player loses a point if he returns the ball so that it hits the ground or a permanent fixture outside his opponent's court.

A player loses a point if he volleys the ball and fails to make a good return, even if standing outside his own court when volleying.

A player loses a point if he deliberately carries or catches the ball on the racket or deliberately hits the ball twice. The key word here is *deliberate*.

The ball is out. This player loses the point even though she was standing off court when she made her volley.

Double hit. This player loses the point.

The player has touched the net with his racket. He loses the point.

It doesn't matter if the ball was going over the net or not: if the player touches the net, she loses the point.

A player loses a point if he or his racket (in hand or otherwise) or anything he is wearing or carrying touches anything pertaining to the net or touches the ground within his opponent's court while the ball is in play.

A player loses a point if he volleys the ball before it passes over the net into his or her court.

A player's racket has landed in his opponent's court. The player who lost the racket loses the point.

A player loses a point if the ball in play touches him or anything he is wearing or carrying other than the racket or his hands holding it. This includes anything the player was wearing or carrying when the point was begun except for the ball used in a first service fault, which may be lying on the court. This means that if you get hit by the ball, no matter how much it may hurt, you lose the point. You lose the point even if play must be suspended while you recover.

The ball must pass over the net before it can be played. This player loses the point.

This player loses the point.

A player loses a point if he throws his racket at and hits the ball.
A player loses a point if he deliberately changes the shape of his racket during the playing of the point.

This player loses the point.

A player loses a point if he hinders an opponent with a deliberate action. Although this need not be a deliberate attempt to hinder, any deliberate action that hinders is sufficient. These actions can range from Harlem Globetrotter–like pyrotechnics on the court to a flamboyant discard of the unused second service ball or loud advice to a doubles partner. The point is, if you distract your opponents, you lose the point.

A player loses the point if he or she hinders the other player.

The point is over and she has lost it.

Unintended hindrances, however, such as screaming when being stung by a wasp or inadvertently brushing an opponent during a frantic exchange of volleys at the net will result in a let.

A player loses the point if the ball strikes a permanent fixture after it has landed in his court. That is, the player who last hit the ball wins the point. (Remember that if singles sticks are in use on a doubles court, the original posts become "permanent fixtures.")

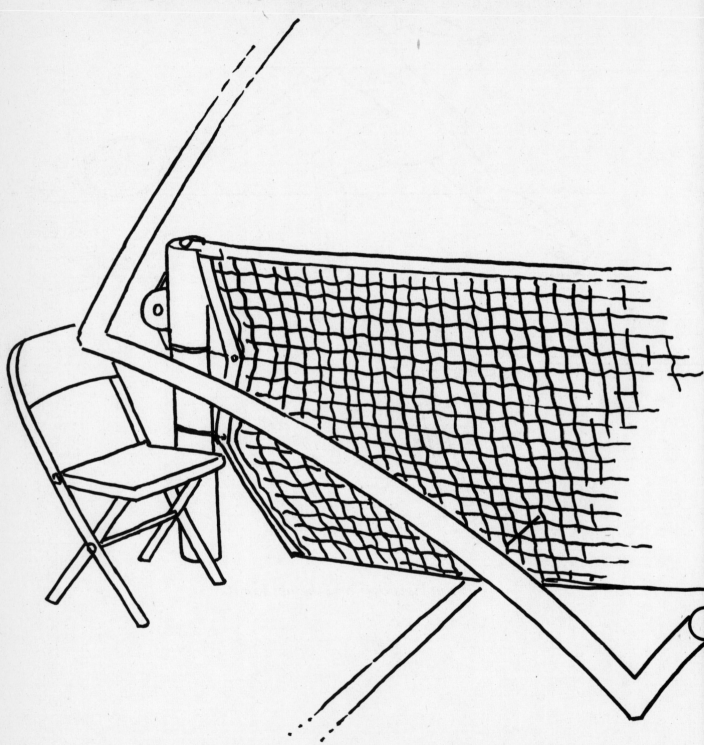

The player who last hit this ball loses the point because the ball hit a permanent fixture before landing in his opponent's court.

SCORING

Games

It doesn't take an accountant to figure out tennis scoring. Four points makes a game, but only if someone is ahead by two points. You keep playing until someone does pull ahead by two points. The 1986 USTA rule book reads: "If a player wins his first point, the score is called 15 for that player; on winning his second point, the score is called 30 for that player; on winning his third point, the score is called 40 for that player; and the fourth point won by a player is scored game. [But] if both players have won three points, the score is called deuce; and the next point . . . is scored advantage for that player. If the same player wins the next point, he wins the game; if the other player wins the next point the score is again called deuce; and so on, until a player wins the two points immediately following the score at deuce; when the game is then won."

Set

The USTA rule book reads: "A player (or players) who first wins six games wins a set; except that he must win by a margin of two games over his opponent and where necessary a set is extended until this margin is achieved." In other words, just as you must win your games by a margin of two points, you must win your sets by two games.

There's an alternative tie-break system described in the appendix of this book (pages 79–80).

Match

The maximum number of sets in a match is five (three for women).

In a three-set match you could lose the first set 6–0, then come back and win the next two sets 9–7 and 6–4. Your opponent has won 17 games to your 15, yet you've won two out of three sets and leave the court the winner of the match.

PACING

In tournament play rest periods, breaks, changes of court, or departures from the court are strictly regulated. Age, sex, and weather are all taken into account in determining what the regulations will be. The following rules will help you pace your game:

- the server should not delay between first and second service;
- the receiver should be ready to respond to the reasonable pace of the server;
- players should take a maximum of a minute and a half between games;
- play is never suspended to allow a player to regain stamina;
- play may be suspended for an injury or for other factors outside the control of the players;
- after the third set for men or the second set for women, a ten-minute rest period is allowable.

*Play should not be stopped
to allow this player to recover.*

Play will be stopped if this player is seriously injured.

TOURNAMENT PLAY

Umpires and Referees

In tournament games, an umpire may be appointed and his decisions are final on points of fact. Points of fact include determining whether the

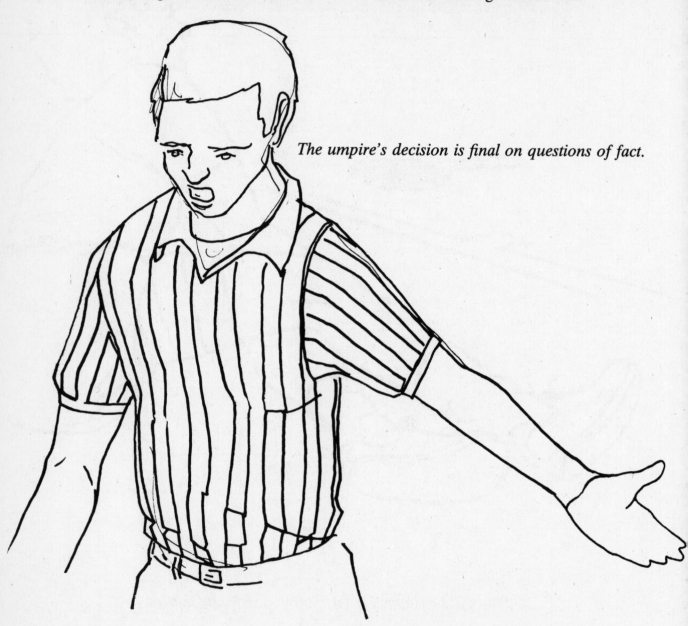

The umpire's decision is final on questions of fact.

ball was in or out, touched the net on serve, etc. He may also overrule any assistants he may have (line judges, net judges, foot-fault judges) if he is sure an error has been made and he overrules immediately. In the case of a hindrance he may also overrule after the point is over. In overruling he may change the decision or order that a let be played. The umpire may also suspend or delay play at any time he deems appropriate.

As a player, you must accept the fact that an umpire cannot overrule an assistant on the basis of an appeal by a player.

If the tournament has also appointed a referee, the umpire's decisions may be appealed to him on questions of law. In team competitions such as the Davis Cup, he may also rule on questions of fact.

The referee may postpone a match because of darkness or bad weather. When the match is resumed, the score at the point of postponement will stand.

The referee may postpone a match for darkness or bad weather. The score will stand unless it is unanimously agreed otherwise.

Coaches

Except when changing ends during a team competition, a player may not receive coaching, advice, or instruction of any kind while on court during a match. After due warning a player may be disqualified from the tournament.

Coaching is highly restricted. This is illegal coaching.

Ball Change

The balls used in a match may be changed after a specified number of games.

DOUBLES

Generally speaking, the rules that apply to singles apply to the doubles game as well. Of course, the court is bigger and the baseline from which service may be struck is longer. The service court, however, is the same size. The main problem in doubles is regulating the order in which the players do things.

Order of Service

After the toss, the pair who will serve in the first game of each set decides which partner will actually be serving that game. The opposing duo decides similarly for the second game. The partner of the player who served the first game serves the third. The partner of the player who served the second serves the fourth, and so on. Let's look at some players: Roger and Roxanne are opposing Suzannah and Stewart. Roger serves the first game; Stewart the second; Roxanne the third; and Suzannah the fourth. Then the cycle starts again. If the set ends in the middle of the cycle, the cycle starts anew with the next set. Or the foursome could establish a new cycle, which they would then adhere to for that set.

Order of Receiving

The pair who will receive service in the first game decides which partner will receive the service for the first point, and that partner will receive first service in every odd game throughout the set. The opposing pair does the same for the second game and continues accordingly. Partners receive service alternately throughout the game. The server's partner and receiver's partner may stand anywhere they like on their own side of the net.

Errors in Order

If an error in serving order is made the mistake should be fixed immediately, but the score, including any faults, stands. However, if the players realize an error in receiving order, they should not rectify it until the end of the game.

Some Rules to Remember

You and your partner are not required to play the ball alternately.

If you both strike the ball when returning it, you will lose the point. The mere clashing of rackets does not count as a double hit.

If you strike your partner with the ball during play you will lose the point.

The doubles service court.

LEGAL SERVING AREA

This is not a double hit; the ball is in play.

This doubles team loses the point.

If you strike your partner with the serve it will be a service fault.

If your partner fails to show up for a doubles tournament, you will be disqualified; you are not allowed to take on your opponents single-handedly.

PART II: TECHNIQUES

THE GRIP

To a great extent, a proper grip will determine the power and control you are able to develop. The grip is the interface between you and your racket, and it is very important. The most common grips are the Eastern forehand, the Eastern backhand, and the Continental, which is a compromise between the first two and a good service and volleying grip. The Western grip is not generally used. It is important to use the free hand between shots to support the racket, holding it at the throat. This rests the racket hand and helps in changing grips.

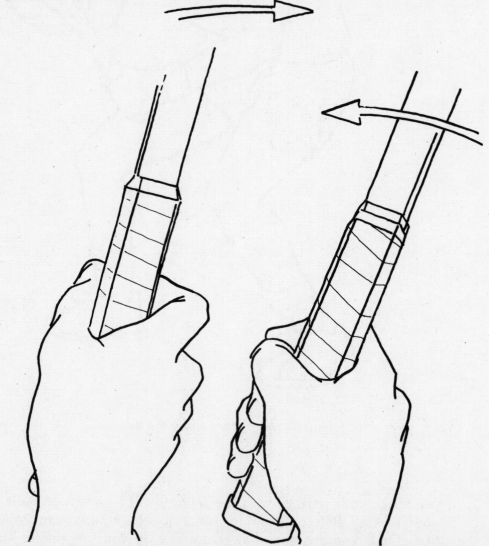

Left: the Eastern backhand grip. Right: the Eastern forehand grip.

THE SERVICE

The service is the single most important stroke in tennis. It may be categorized into three types: flat (no rotation on the ball), slice, and spin. Although a flat service is ultimately the most difficult to hit with accuracy and power and a spin service is easier to control for the experienced player, a moderately paced flat service is the easiest with which to learn the basic service stroke.

The service: weight is mostly on the back foot.

Ultimately, all parts of a stroke should blend into a single, fluid motion rather than remain separate parts, as the stroke is described here. (The instructions in this book are given for right-handed players; southpaws should make the appropriate reversals.)

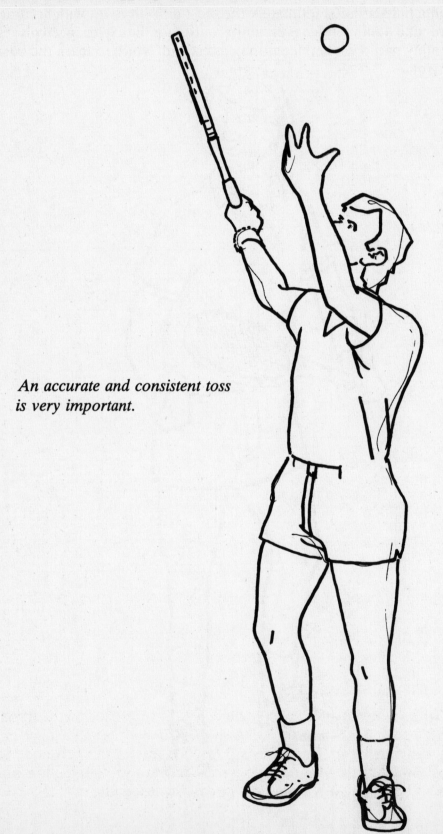

An accurate and consistent toss is very important.

*The racket starts forward
as the ball is reaching its highest point.*

*Hit the ball at its highest point when
it momentarily becomes stationary.*

Begin with the racket held in the right hand and supported on the throat by the left hand. Keep your arms close to your body and your weight primarily on your right (back) foot. Begin the toss of the ball and the racket backswing while shifting your weight forward so that you are balanced on both feet equally. An accurate, consistent toss is one of the most important goals for a beginner. Start the racket forward from a cocked position behind the head as the ball is reaching its highest point. The ball should be struck at its maximum height about two feet in front of the body. Snap your wrist forward and direct the racket head where you want the ball to go. Your weight will have continued to shift and will now be primarily on your left foot. Your follow-through should naturally bring you in to an approximation of the ready position.

Imagine on the follow-through that you are throwing the racket where you want the ball to go.

THE READY POSITION

The ready position is the stance to assume after every shot. It is the ideal, balanced stance from which to move forward, left, or right rapidly and be able to react to the ball quickly. Remain loose and poised with

The ready position.

Move to the ball while getting the racket back early.

your weight forward on the balls of your feet with your knees slightly bent. The racket should be held in the middle of the body, its head about midriff height and cradled in the left hand at the throat, as well as held in the right by the grip. In moving toward the ball during baseline volleys, take rapid short strides *and get the racket back for the swing as early as possible.*

FOREHAND

The forehand is the first stroke learned by most people. It is the most common stroke in the game and fortunately the easiest to master. It may be hit flat or with spin.

The forehand:
getting ready to step forward with the left foot.

Transfer your weight back as the racket moves back.

To hit the forehand, step forward with your left foot while pivoting your right foot. Bring your shoulders perpendicular to the net. Take your racket back as your weight is transferred onto your right foot.

As your arm straightens, shift your weight forward.

As your racket begins to move forward under the ball, straighten your elbow and then your wrist as you shift your weight onto the left foot. When you hit the ball, put your entire body into the stroke. It will increase your power dramatically. The straight wrist and elbow break as you follow through, and the racket naturally ends up on the left side of the body, above the head.

The right shoulder should be well down.

Use your whole body for power.

BACKHAND

If you can throw a Frisbee, you can develop a fine backhand. With practice, you can use topspin or slice and eventually hit it as powerfully as a forehand. In one sense the backhand is even easier to learn than the forehand because moving the right arm across the body encourages the proper stance.

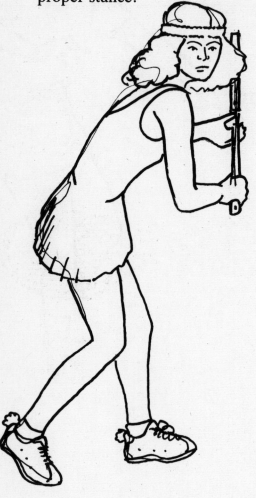

The backhand:
let your left arm pull the racket back.

Step forward with your right foot.

The swing starts high but moves straight through the ball.

From the ready position, the racket is pulled back by the left arm as the left foot pivots. As the racket and the left arm move, pivot your body to the left and step forward with your right foot. The swing starts high and, as the arm straightens out, arcs straight through the ball. At this point, the right shoulder should be well down. Allow the racket to follow through naturally, high and to the right side of the body. Just as with the other strokes, as you execute it, your weight should be transferred from the back to the front foot. Use your whole body for power.

Your body weight moves forward.

FOREHAND AND BACKHAND VOLLEYS

When at the net, always anticipate an opportunity to volley. Wait for the return in a ready position two to three yards inside the service court. Hold your racket high in a Continental grip. When the ball is hit, quickly

The short forehand volley:
take a small step toward the ball;
use a short follow-through.

decide whether to attempt a forehand or a backhand stroke and take a short oblique step toward the ball (the left foot if forehand, right if backhand). This step should begin to bring your shoulders perpendicular to the net. Things happen fast at the net and the most successful volleyers are those who work quickly and efficiently. The backswing is minimal,

Short backswing: take a small step toward the ball; use a short follow-through.

and a short sharp punching motion is used in both the forehand and backhand volleys and follow-throughs. After striking the ball, immediately assume a ready position, anticipating that the next ball struck will require a volley.

In hitting low volleys, get to the ball by bending the knees rather than dropping the head of the racket. Keep the racket head high.

Bend the knees on low volleys—don't reach down with the racket.

THE OVERHEAD SMASH

The overhead is usually hit from the service courts, and if it is well hit it will be a winner. The overhead smash is very similar to the service, but the timing of it is more difficult. For these reasons, you should concentrate on hitting it well, rather than on excessive power or pinpoint placement.

The overhead smash: stand slightly behind the ball.

Straighten the body.

Hit the ball at the highest point possible.

Follow through for power.

Take a slightly crouched position, a little behind where the ball is coming down. Bring the racket and free hand up at the same time as you straighten the body. Begin your swing behind the head and strike the ball at its highest point. As with other strokes, shift your weight forward for power. Finish with a full follow-through and assume the ready position.

DROP AND LOB

Dropping the ball in your opponent's court just over the net or lobbing it over his head can be an extremely effective shot in the right circumstances. The two most important things to remember about the drop shot and the lob are that they work well in combination and that they depend on surprise for their effectiveness. So don't "telegraph" these shots. Hit the drop shot with a backspin, chopping motion. It should clear the net with a reasonable margin of error. It should land within three yards of the net and have enough backspin to die there. It's not an easy shot to hit.

The drop shot requires a short chopping stroke to create backspin so that the ball will "die."

*This lob shot has been disguised
to look like a normal backswing.*

Place the lob as near to the baseline as is reasonably possible. The preparatory backswing should look just like the backswing for a drive. Hit an offensive lob when your opponent is at the net expecting to volley. It should be just high enough so that he can't reach it. The ball should have some topspin so that it bounds away from your opponent. Hit a defensive lob higher, with backspin to buy time to get back into position.

TENNIS TACTICS

To play winning tennis, or even to have fun at it, good technique is indispensable. It is equally important to employ sound tactical principles. The beginner in tennis should first work to play a steady game and eliminate his unforced errors. He should allow himself a margin of error on shots and not try to hit fireball shots with perfect on-the-line placement. Rather, he should keep the ball alive and force his opponent to come up with something that will beat him. As his skill improves he will naturally begin to take advantage of opportunities for "winners" and finally begin to create them.

If during the warm-up or during play you discover that your opponent has a technical weakness, don't get greedy and play to it the whole match—that will just give him a chance to practice and improve it. Exploit the weakness when you need to win key points. However, if your opponent has a stamina problem, exploit that at every opportunity; make him run, run, run.

Service

When serving, concentrate on getting your first service in instead of making an "ace." Aim inside the far corner to open up the court for an approach shot or the near corner to keep your opponent honest or to exploit a stroke weakness. On the second service try to serve deep to the backhand. Don't serve up a turkey just to get it in.

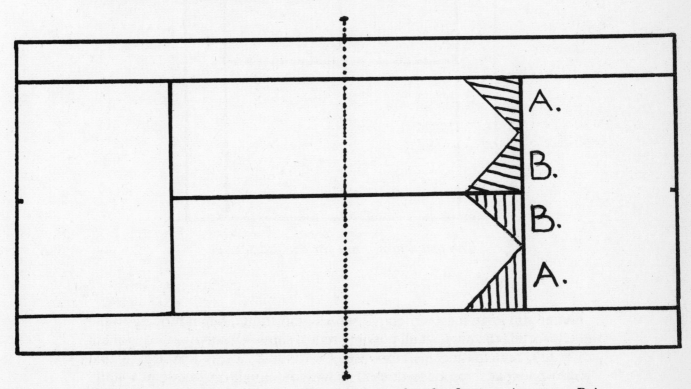

The service: area A is the usual aim point for the first service; area B is used to keep the opponent guessing.

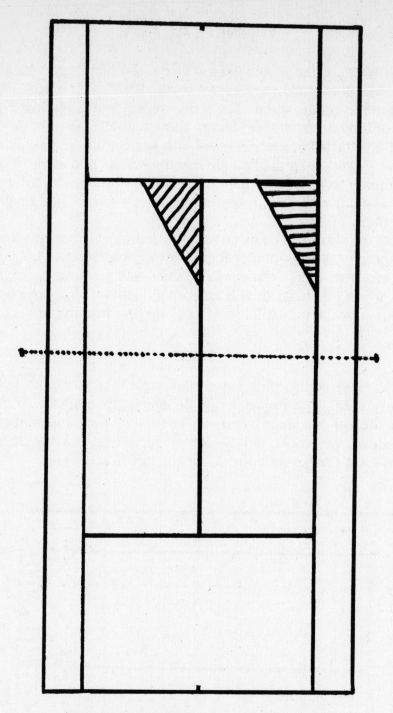

The usual aim point for second service.

After you have hit an effective service you should begin moving to the net, bisecting the angle of all possible return shots. Observe your opponent carefully, anticipating his response. Continue to press forward so that your opponent's response doesn't leave you caught in "no-man's-land" (halfway to the net). Attack the ball for an approach volley, and then move to the net for the kill.

Returning Service

It's not easy to make a good return of service, but if you can, the odds of your winning the point are enormously improved. When returning service, begin by assuming a proper ready position, taking your stance as close to the net as is reasonably possible. This will lessen the amount of ground you must cover laterally. Return the service somehow, at all costs, no matter how difficult.

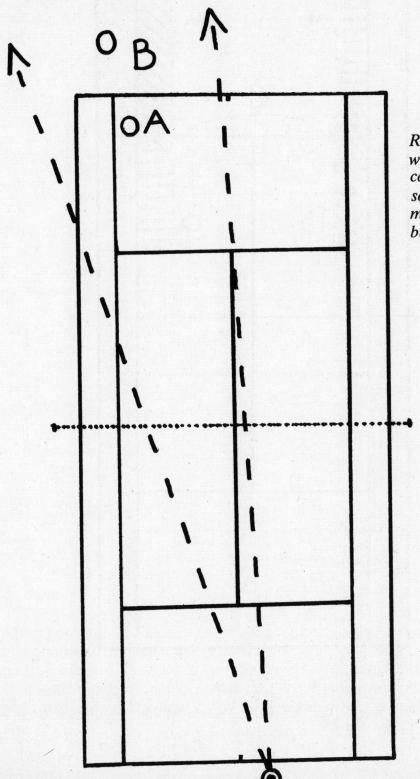

Returning serve: player A will have less ground to cover to get to and return service; player B will have more time to get to the serve, but more ground to cover.

Against a server rushing the net, return crosscourt or down the line. Get to the ball as soon as possible to cut down on the server's approach time and force a poor shot. Against a baseline player, be sure the ball is returned deep. During the rally, probe and run your opponent; syncopate

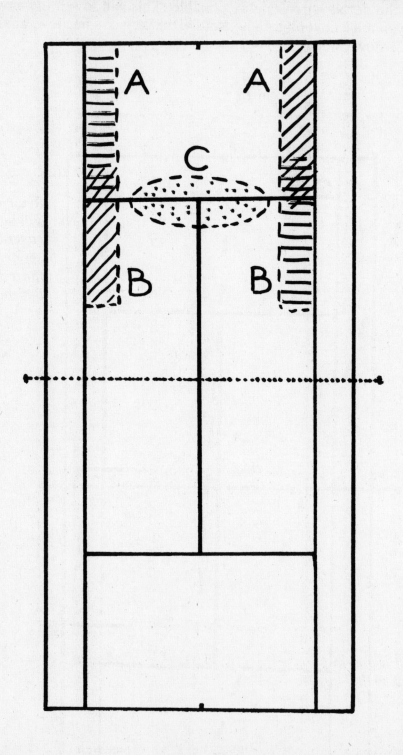

Against a net-rushing server, hit the ball down the line (A) or across court (B), or hit it at his feet (C) to force a weak return.

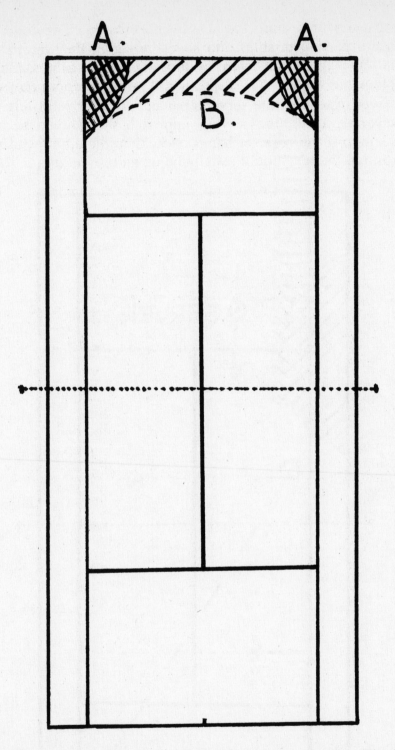

Against a baseline player, hit the ball deep at all costs (B). The best spot to hit is in the corners (A).

the direction and pace of your shots. If you receive a shot down the line, it is generally a good idea to return it crosscourt. It's still a must to turn the tables and get to the net whenever a reasonable chance presents itself.

Doubles Tactics

If you are playing doubles and have the serve, the way to win is to bring the server to the net (with his partner) as soon as possible and stay there unless forced back. The receiver will probably try to return the ball to the server instead of the server's partner. If after returning the serve the receiver advances, the server's approach shot should be hit at the receiver's feet. If the receiver hangs back, then the approach shot of the server rushing the net should usually be down the middle.

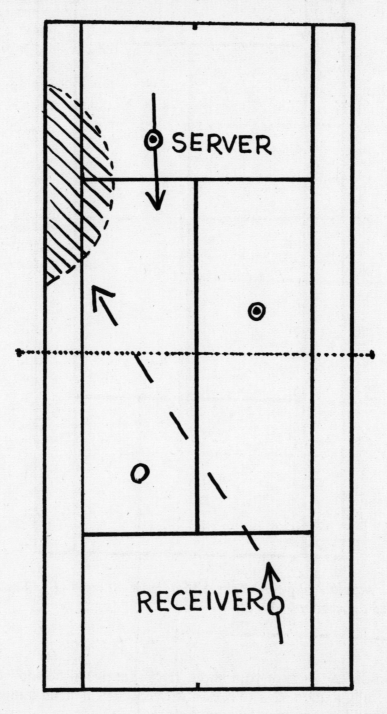

In doubles, return service across court.

It is very difficult to return service in doubles. Just as in singles, immediate loss of the point should be avoided and the ball should be returned at all costs. The ball should be returned as early as possible. Hit it low and crosscourt to buy time and avoid the net-guarding partner. Some helpful guidelines for playing doubles are:

- Cover for your partner when he is pulled out of position by a sharply angled return.
- Balls down the middle should be taken by the player who can reach the ball with his forehand.
- Balls hit crosscourt should be taken by the player diagonally opposite the court it was hit from.
- During a point-blank exchange, the player who last hit the ball should continue to play it if both partners have an equal chance.

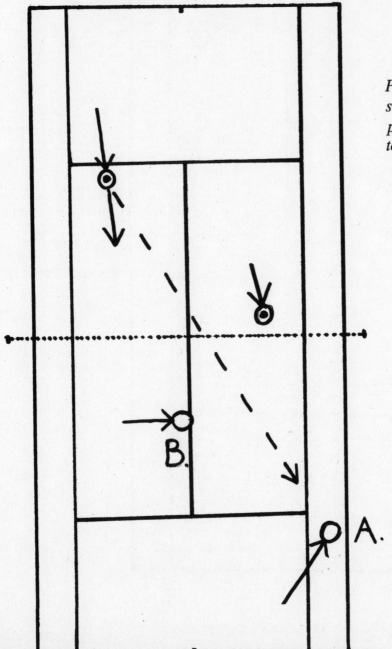

Player A has had to chase a sharply angled ball and player B has moved to cover for him.

RULES OF TENNIS AND CASES AND DECISIONS 1986
Reprinted with permission from the United States Tennis Association.

The following Rules and Cases and Decisions are the official Code of the International Tennis Federation, of which the United States Tennis Association is a member. USTA Comments and USTA Cases and Decisions have the same weight and force in USTA tournaments as do ITF Cases and Decisions.

When a match is played without officials the principles and guidelines set forth in the USTA Publication, The Code, shall apply in any situation not covered by the rules.

Except where otherwise stated, every reference in these Rules to the masculine includes the feminine gender.

A vertical line in the margin by a rule indicates a change made by the ITF in July 1985 and which took effect January 1, 1986. A vertical line by a USTA Comment indicates a change made since the last edition.

The Singles Game
RULE 1
The Court

The court shall be a rectangle 78 feet (23.77m.) long and 27 feet (8.23m.) wide. **USTA Comment:** See Rule 34 for a doubles court.

It shall be divided across the middle by a net suspended from a cord or metal cable of a maximum diameter of one-third of an inch (0.8cm.), the ends of which shall be attached to, or pass over, the tops of two posts, which shall be not more than 6 inches (15cm.) square or 6 inches (15cm.) in diameter. The centres of the posts shall be 3 feet (0.914m.) outside the court on each side and the height of the posts shall be such that the top of the cord or metal cable shall be 3 feet 6 inches (1.07m.) above the ground.

When a combined doubles (see Rule 34) and singles court with a doubles net is used for singles, the net must be supported to a height of 3 feet 6 inches (1.07m.) by means of two posts, called "singles sticks", which shall be not more than 3 inches (7.5cm.) square or 3 inches (7.5cm.) in diameter. The centres of the singles sticks shall be 3 feet (0.914m.) outside the singles court on each side.

The net shall be extended fully so that it fills completely the space between the two posts and shall be of sufficiently small mesh to prevent the ball passing through. The height of the net shall be 3 feet (0.914m) at the centre, where it shall be held down taut by a strap not more than 2 inches (5cm.) wide and completely white in colour. There shall be a band covering the cord or metal cable and the top of the net of not less than 2 inches (5cm.) nor more than 2½ inches (6.3cm.) in depth on each side and completely white in colour.

There shall be no advertisement on the net, strap, band or singles sticks.

The lines bounding the ends and sides of the Court shall respectively be called the base-lines and the side-lines. On each side of the net, at a distance of 21 feet (6.40m.) from it and parallel with it, shall be drawn the service-lines. The space on each side of the net between the service-line and the side-lines shall be divided into two equal parts called the service-courts by the centre service-line, which must be 2 inches (5cm.) in width, drawn half-way between, and parallel with, the side-lines. Each base-line shall be bisected by an imaginary continuation of the centre service-line to a line 4 inches (10cm.) in length and 2 inches (5cm.) in width called the centre mark drawn inside the Court, at right angles to and in contact with such base-lines. All other lines shall be not less than 1 inch (2.5cm.) nor more than 2 inches (5cm.) in width, except the base-line, which may be 4 inches (10cm.) in width, and all measurements shall be made to the outside of the lines. All lines shall be of uniform colour.

If advertising or any other material is placed at the back of the court, it may not contain white or yellow, or any other light colour.

If advertisements are placed on the chairs of the Linesmen sitting at the back of the court, they may not contain white or yellow.

Note: In the case of the International Tennis Championship (Davis Cup) or other Official Championships of the International Tennis Federation, there shall be a space behind each base-line of not less than 21 feet (6.4m.), and at the sides of not less than 12 feet (3.66m.).

USTA Comment: *It is important to have a stick 3 feet, 6 inches long, with a notch cut in at the 3-foot mark for the purpose of measuring the height of the net at the posts and in the center. These measurements always should be made before starting to play a match.*

RULE 2
Permanent Fixtures

The permanent fixtures of the Court shall include not only the net, posts, singles sticks, cord or metal cable, strap and band, but also, where there are any such, the back and side stops, the stands, fixed or movable seats and chairs round the Court, and their occupants, all other fixtures around and above the Court, and the Umpire, Net-cord Judge, Foot-fault Judge, Linesmen and Ball Boys when in their respective places.

Note: For the purpose of this Rule, the word "Umpire" comprehends the Umpire, the persons entitled to a seat on the Court, and all those persons designated to assist the Umpire in the conduct of a match.

RULE 3
The Ball

The ball shall have a uniform outer surface and shall be white or yellow in colour. If there are any seams, they shall be stitchless.

The ball shall be more than two and a half inches (6.35cm.) and less than two and five-eighths inches (6.67cm.) in diameter, and more than two ounces (56.7 grams) and less than two and one-sixteenth ounces (58.5 grams) in weight.

The ball shall have a bound of more than 53 inches (135cm.) and less than 58 inches (147cm.) when dropped 100 inches (254cm.) upon a concrete base.

The ball shall have a forward deformation of more than .220 of an inch (.56cm.) and less than .290 of an inch (.74cm.) and a return deformation of more than .350 of an inch (.89cm.) and less than .425 of an inch (1.08cm.) at 18 lb. (8.165kg.) load. The two deformation figures shall be the averages of three individual readings along three axes of the ball and no two individual readings shall differ by more than .030 of an inch (.08cm.) in each case.

All tests for bound, size and deformation shall be made in accordance with the Regulations in the Appendix hereto.

RULE 4
The Racket

Rackets failing to comply with the following specifications are not approved for play under the Rules of Tennis:

(a) The hitting surface of the racket shall be flat and consist of a pattern of crossed strings connected to a frame and alternately interlaced or bonded where they cross; and the stringing pattern shall be generally uniform, and in particular not less dense in the centre than in any other area. The strings shall be free of attached objects and protrusions other than those utilized soley and specifically to limit or prevent wear and tear or vibration and which are reasonable in size and placement for such purposes.

(b) The frame of the racket shall not exceed 32 inches (81.28cm.) in overall length, including the handle and 12½ inches (31.75cm.) in overall width. The strung surface shall not exceed 15½ inches (39.37cm.) in overall length, and 11½ inches (29.21cm.) in overall width.

(c) The frame, including the handle, shall be free of attached objects and devices other than those utilized solely and specifically to limit or prevent wear and tear or vibration, or to distribute weight. Any objects and devices must be reasonable in size and placement for such purposes.

(d) The frame, including the handle and the strings, shall be free of any device which makes it possible to change materially the shape of the racket, or to change the weight distribution, during the playing of a point.

The International Tennis Federation shall rule on the question of whether any racket or prototype complies with the above specifications or is otherwise approved, or not approved, for play. Such ruling may be undertaken on its own initiative, or upon application by any party with a bona fide interest therein, including any player, equipment manufacturer or National Association or members thereof. Such rulings and applications shall be made in accordance with the applicable Review and Hearing Procedures of the International Tennis Federation, copies of which may be obtained from the office of the Secretary.

Case 1. Can there be more than one set of strings on the hitting surface of a racket?
Decision. No. The rule clearly mentions a pattern, and not patterns, of crossed strings.
Case 2. Is the stringing pattern of a racket considered to be generally uniform and flat if the strings are of a different gauge?
Decision. No.
Case 3. Is the stringing pattern of a racket considered to be generally uniform and flat if the strings are on more than one plane?
Decision. No.

RULE 5
Server and Receiver
The players shall stand on opposite sides of the net; the player who first delivers the ball shall be called the Server, and the other the Receiver.

Case 1. Does a player, attempting a stroke, lose the point if he crosses an imaginary line in the extension of the net,
   (a) before striking the ball,
   (b) after striking the ball?
Decision. He does not lose the point in either case by crossing the imaginary line and provided he does not enter the lines bounding his opponent's Court (Rule 20 (e)). In regard to hindrance, his opponent may ask for the decision of the Umpire under Rules 21 and 25.
Case 2. The Server claims that the Receiver must stand within the lines bounding his Court. Is this necessary?
Decision. No. The Receiver may stand wherever he pleases on his own side of the net.

RULE 6
Choice of Ends and Service
The choice of ends and the right to be Server or Receiver in the first game shall be decided by toss. The player winning the toss may choose or require his opponent to choose:
   (a) The right to be Server or Receiver, in which case the other player shall choose the end; or
   (b) The end, in which case the other player shall choose the right to be Server or Receiver.

USTA Comment: *These choices should be made promptly and are irrevocable.*

RULE 7
The Service
The service shall be delivered in the following manner. Immediately before commencing to serve, the Server shall stand with both feet at rest behind (i.e. further from the net than) the base-line, and within the imaginary continuations of the centre-mark and side-line. The Server shall then project the ball by hand into the air in any direction and before it hits the ground strike it with his racket, and the delivery shall be deemed to have been completed at the moment of the impact of the racket and the ball. A player with the use of only one arm may utilize his racket for the projection.

USTA Comment: *The service begins when the Server takes a ready position and ends when his racket makes contact with the ball, or when he misses the ball in attempting to serve it.*

Case 1. May the Server in a singles game take his stand behind the portion of the base-line between the side-lines of the Singles Court and the Doubles Court?
Decision. No.
Case 2. If a player, when serving, throws up two or more balls instead of one, does he lose that service?
Decision. No. A let should be called, but if the Umpire regards the action as deliberate he may take action under Rule 21.
USTA Case 3. May a player serve underhand?
Decision. Yes. There is no restriction regarding the kind of service which may be used; that is, the player may use an underhand or overhand service at his discretion.

RULE 8
Foot Fault
(a) The Server shall throughout the delivery of the service:
   (i) Not change his position by walking or running. The Server shall not by slight movements of the feet which do not materially afect the location originally taken up by him, be deemed "to change his position by walking or running".
   (ii) Not touch, with either foot, any area other than that behind the base-line within the imaginary extensions of the centre mark and side-lines.

(b) The word "foot" means the extremity of the leg below the ankle.

USTA Comment: *This rule covers the most decisive stroke in the game, and there is no justification for its not being obeyed by players and enforced by officials. No official has the right to instruct any umpire to disregard violations of it. In a non-officiated match, it is the prerogative of the Receiver, or his partner, to call foot faults, but only after all efforts (appeal to the server, requests for an umpire, etc.) have failed and the foot faulting is so flagrant as to be clearly perceptible from the Receiver's side.*

RULE 9
Delivery of Service
(a) In delivering the service, the Server shall stand alternately behind the right and left Courts beginning from the right in every game. If service from a wrong half of the Court occurs and is undetected, all play resulting from such wrong service or services shall stand, but the inaccuracy of station shall be corrected immediately it is discovered.

(b) The ball served shall pass over the net and hit the ground within the Service Court which is diagonally opposite, or upon any line bounding such Court, before the Receiver returns it.

RULE 10
Service Fault
The Service is a fault:
   (a) If the Server commits any breach of Rules 7, 8 or 9;
   (b) If he misses the ball in attempting to strike it;
   (c) If the ball served touches a permanent fixture (other than the net, strap or band) before it hits the ground.

Case 1. After throwing a ball up preparatory to serving, the Server decides not to strike at it and catches it instead. Is it a fault?
Decision. No. **USTA Comment:** As long as the Server makes no attempt to strike the ball, it is immaterial whether he catches it in his hand or on his racket or lets it drop to the ground.
Case 2. In serving in a singles game played on a Doubles Court with doubles posts and singles sticks, the ball hits a singles stick and then hits the ground within the lines of the correct Service Court. Is this a fault or a let?
Decision. In serving it is a fault, because the singles stick, the doubles post, and that portion of the net, or band between them are permanent fixtures. (Rules 2 and 10, and note to Rule 24.).

USTA Comment: *The significant point governing Case 2 is that the part of the net and band "outside" the singles sticks is not part of the net over which this singles match is being played. Thus such a serve is a fault under the provisions of Article (c) above... By the same token, this would be a fault also if it were a singles game played with permanent posts in the singles position. (See Case 1 under Rule 24 for difference between "service" and "good return" with respect to a ball's hitting a net post.)*

USTA Comment: *In matches played without umpires each player makes calls for all balls hit to his side of the net. In doubles, normally the Receiver's partner makes the calls with respect to the service line, with the Receiver calling the side and center lines, but either partner may make the call on any ball he clearly sees out.*

RULE 11
Second Service
After a fault (if it is the first fault) the Server shall serve again from behind the same half of the Court from which he served that fault, unless the service was from the wrong half, when, in accordance with Rule 9, the Server shall be entitled to one service only from behind the other half.

Case 1. A player serves from a wrong Court. He loses the point and then claims it was a fault because of his wrong station.
Decision. The point stands as played and the next service should be from the correct station according to the score.
Case 2. The point score being 15 all, the Server, by mistake, serves from the left-hand Court. He wins the point. He then serves again from the right-hand Court, delivering a fault. This mistake in station is then discovered. Is he entitled to the previous point? From which Court should he next serve?
Decision. The previous point stands. The next service should be from the left-hand Court, the score being 30/15, and the Server has served one fault.

RULE 12
When To Serve
The Server shall not serve until the Receiver is ready. If the latter attempts to return the service, he shall be deemed ready. If, however, the Receiver signifies that he is not ready, he may not claim a fault

because the ball does not hit the ground within the limits fixed for the service.

USTA Comment: *The Server must wait until the Receiver is ready for the second service as well as the first, and if the Receiver claims to be not ready and does not make any effort to return a service, the Server may not claim the point, even though the service was good. However, the Receiver, having indicated he is ready, may not become unready unless some outside interference takes place.*

RULE 13
The Let
In all cases where a let has to be called under the rules, or to provide for an interruption to play, it shall have the following interpretations:
(a) When called solely in respect of a service that one service only shall be replayed.
(b) When called under any other circumstance, the point shall be replayed.

USTA Comment: *A service that touches the net in passing yet falls into the proper court (or touches the receiver) is a let. This word is used also when, because of an interruption while the ball is in play, or for any other reason, a point is to be replayed. A spectator's outcry (of "out", "fault" or other) is not a valid basis for replay of a point, but action should be taken to prevent a recurrence.*

Case 1. A service is interrupted by some cause outside those defined in Rule 14. Should the service only be replayed?
Decision. No, the whole point must be replayed.

USTA Comment: *If a service delay is caused by the Receiver or by an official the whole point shall be replayed; if the delay is caused by the Server, the Server has one serve to come.*

USTA Comment: *The phrase "in respect of a service" in (a) means a let because a served ball has touched the net before landing in the proper court, OR because the Receiver was not ready . . . Case 1 refers to a second serve, and the decision means that if the interruption occurs during delivery of the second service, the Server gets two serves. Example: On a second service a linesman calls "fault" and immediately corrects it (the Receiver meanwhile having let the ball go by). The Server is entitled to two serves, on this ground: The corrected call means that the Server has put the ball into play with a good service, and once the ball is in play and a let is called, the point must be replayed . . . Note, however, that if the serve is an unmistakable ace — that is, the Umpire is sure the erroneous call had no part in the Receiver's inability to play the ball — the point should be declared for the Server.*

Case 2. If a ball in play becomes broken, should a let be called?
Decision. Yes.

USTA Comment: *A ball shall be regarded as having become "broken" if, in the opinion of the Chair Umpire, it is found to have lost compression to the point of being unfit for further play, or unfit for any reason, and it is clear the defective ball was the one in play.*

RULE 14
The "Let" in Service
The service is a let:
(a) If the ball served touches the net, strap or band, and is otherwise good, or, after touching the net, strap or band, touches the Receiver or anything which he wears or carries before hitting the ground.
(b) If a service or a fault is delivered when the Receiver is not ready (see Rule 12).

In case of a let, that particular service shall not count, and the Server shall serve again, but a service let does not annul a previous fault.

RULE 15
Order of Service
At the end of the first game the Receiver shall become Server, and the Server Receiver; and so on alternately in all the subsequent games of a match. If a player serves out of turn, the player who ought to have served shall serve as soon as the mistake is discovered, but all points scored before such discovery shall be reckoned. If a game shall have been completed before such discovery, the order of service remains as altered. A fault served before such discovery shall not be reckoned.

RULE 16
When Players Change Ends
The players shall change ends at the end of the first, third and every subsequent alternate game of each set, and at the end of each set unless the total number of games in such set is even, in which case the change is not made until the end of the first game of the next set.

If a mistake is made and the correct sequence is not followed the players must take up their correct station as soon as the discovery is made and follow their original sequence.

RULE 17
The Ball in Play
A ball is in play from the moment at which it is delivered in service. Unless a fault or a let is called it remains in play until the point is decided.

USTA Comment: *A point is not decided simply when, or because, a good shot has clearly passed a player, or when an apparently bad shot passes over a baseline or sideline. An outgoing ball is still definitely in play until it actually strikes the ground, backstop or a permanent fixture (other than the net, posts, singles sticks, cord or metal cable, strap or band), or a player. The same applies to a good ball, bounding after it has landed in the proper court. A ball that becomes imbedded in the net is out of play.*

Case 1. A player fails to make a good return. No call is made and the ball remains in play. May his opponent later claim the point after the rally has ended?
Decision. No. The point may not be claimed if the players continue to play after the error has been made, provided the opponent was not hindered.

USTA Comment: *To be valid, an out call on A's shot to B's court, that B plays, must be made before B's shot has either gone out of play or has been hit by A. See Case 3 under Rule 29.*

USTA Case 2. A ball is played into the net; the player on the other side, thinking that the ball is coming over, strikes at it and hits the net. Who loses the point?
Decision. If the player touched the net while the ball was still in play, he loses the point.

RULE 18
Server Wins Point
The Server wins the point:
(a) If the ball served, not being a let under Rule 14, touches the Receiver or anything which he wears or carries, before it hits the ground;
(b) If the Receiver otherwise loses the point as provided by Rule 20.

RULE 19
Receiver Wins Point
The Receiver wins the point:
(a) If the Server serves two consecutive faults;
(b) If the Server otherwise loses the point as provided by Rule 20.

RULE 20
Player Loses Point
A player loses the point if:
(a) He fails, before the ball in play has hit the ground twice consecutively, to return it directly over the net (except as provided in Rule 24(a) or (c)); or
(b) He returns the ball in play so that it hits the ground, a permanent fixture, or other object, outside any of the lines which bound his opponent's Court (except as provided in Rule 24(a) or (c)); or

USTA Comment: *A ball hitting a scoring device or other object attached to a net post results in loss of point to the striker.*

(c) He volleys the ball and fails to make a good return even when standing outside the Court; or
(d) In playing the ball he deliberately carries or catches it on his racket or deliberately touches it with his racket more than once; or

USTA Comment: *Only when there is a definite "second push" by the player does his shot become illegal, with consequent loss of point. It should be noted that the word "deliberately" is the key word in this Rule and that two hits occurring in the course of a single continuous stroke would not be deemed a double hit.*

(e) He or his racket (in his hand or otherwise) or anything which he wears or carries touches the net, posts, singles sticks, cord or metal cable, strap or band, or the ground within his opponent's Court at any time while the ball is in play; or

USTA Comment: *Touching a pipe support that runs across the*

court at the bottom of the net is interpreted as touching the net; See USTA Comment under Rule 23.

(f) He volleys the ball before it has passed the net; or

(g) The ball in play touches him or anything that he wears or carries, except his racket in his hand or hands: or

USTA Comment: *This loss of point occurs regardless of whether the player is inside or outside the bounds of his court when the ball touches him. Except for a ball used in a first service fault, a player is considered to be "wearing or carrying" anything that he was wearing or carrying at the beginning of the point during which the touch occurred.*

(h) He throws his racket at and hits the ball; or

(i) He deliberately and materially changes the shape of his racket during the playing of the point.

Case 1. In serving, the racket flies from the Server's hand and touches the net before the ball has touched the ground. Is this a fault, or does the player lose the point?

Decision. The Server loses the point because his racket touches the net whilst the ball is in play (Rule 20 *(e)*).

Case 2. In serving, the racket flies from the Server's hand and touches the net after the ball has touched the ground outside the proper court. Is this a fault, or does the player lose the point?

Decision. This is a fault because the ball was out of play when the racket touched the net.

Case 3. A and B are playing against C and D, A is serving to D, C touches the net before the ball touches the ground. A fault is then called because the service falls outside the Service Court. Do C and D lose the point?

Decision. The call "fault" is an erroneous one. C and D had already lost the point before "fault" could be called, because C touched the net whilst the ball was in play (Rule 20 *(e)*).

Case 4. May a player jump over the net into his opponent's Court while the ball is in play and not suffer penalty?

Decision. No. He loses the point (Rule 20 *(e)*).

Case 5. A cuts the ball just over the net, and it returns to A's side. B, unable to reach the ball, throws his racket and hits the ball. Both racket and ball fall over the net on A's Court. A returns the ball outside of B's Court. Does B win or lose the point?

Decision. B loses the point (Rule 20 *(e)* and *(h)*).

Case 6. A player standing outside the service Court is struck by a service ball before it has touched the ground. Does he win or lose the point?

Decision. The player struck loses the point (Rule 20 *(g)*), except as provided under Rule 14 *(a)*.

Case 7. A player standing outside the Court volleys the ball or catches it in his hand and claims the point because the ball was certainly going out of court.

Decision. In no circumstances can he claim the point:

(1) If he catches the ball he loses the point under Rule 20 *(g)*.

(2) If he volleys it and makes a bad return he loses the point under Rule 20 *(c)*.

(3) If he volleys it and makes a good return, the rally continues.

RULE 21
Player Hinders Opponent

If a player commits any act which hinders his opponent in making a stroke, then, if this is deliberate, he shall lose the point or if involuntary, the point shall be replayed.

USTA Comment: *'Deliberate' means a player did what he intended to do, although the resulting effect on his opponent might or might not have been what he intended. Example: a player, after his return is in the air, gives advice to his partner in such a loud voice that his opponent is hindered. 'Involuntary' means a non-intentional act such as a hat blowing off or a scream resulting from a sudden wasp sting.*

Case 1. Is a player liable to a penalty if in making a stroke he touches his opponent?

Decision. No, unless the Umpire deems it necessary to take action under Rule 21.

Case 2. When a ball bounds back over the net, the player concerned may reach over the net in order to play the ball. What is the ruling if the player is hindered from doing this by his opponent?

Decision. In accordance with Rule 21, the Umpire may either award the point to the player hindered, or order the point to be replayed. (See also Rule 25).

Case 3. Does an involuntary double hit constitute an act which hinders an opponent within Rule 21?

Decision. No.

USTA Comment: *Upon appeal by a competitor that an opponent's action in discarding a "second ball" after a rally has started constitutes a distraction (hindrance), the Umpire, if he deems the claim valid, shall require the opponent to make some other and satisfactory disposition of the ball. Failure to comply with this instruction may result in loss of point(s) or disqualification.*

RULE 22
Ball Falls on Line

A ball falling on a line is regarded as falling in the Court bounded by that line.

USTA Comment: *In matches played without officials, it is customary for each player to make the calls on all balls hit to his side of the net, and if a player cannot call a ball out with surety he should regard it as good. See The Code.*

RULE 23
Ball Touches Permanent Fixtures

If the ball in play touches a permanent fixture (other than the net, posts, singles sticks, cord or metal cable, strap or band) after it has hit the ground, the player who struck it wins the point; if before it hits the ground, his opponent wins the point.

Case 1. A return hits the Umpire or his chair or stand. The player claims that the ball was going into Court.

Decision. He loses the point.

USTA Comment: *A ball in play that after passing the net strikes a pipe support running across the court at the base of the net is regarded the same as a ball landing on clear ground. See also Rule 20(e).*

RULE 24
A Good Return

It is a good return:

(a) If the ball touches the net, posts, singles sticks, cord or metal cable, strap or band, provided that it passes over any of them and hits the ground within the Court; or

(b) If the ball, served or returned, hits the ground within the proper Court and rebounds or is blown back over the net, and the player whose turn it is to strike reaches over the net and plays the ball, provided that neither he nor any part of his clothes or racket touches the net, posts, singles sticks, cord or metal cable, strap or band or the ground within his opponent's Court, and that the stroke is otherwise good; or

(c) If the ball is returned outside the posts, or singles sticks, either above or below the level of the top of the net, even though it touches the posts or singles sticks, provided that it hits the ground within the proper Court; or

(d) If a player's racket passes over the net after he has returned the ball, provided the ball passes the net before being played and is properly returned; or

(e) If a player succeeds in returning the ball, served or in play, which strikes a ball lying in the Court.

USTA Comment: *i.e., on his court when the point started; if the ball in play strikes a ball, rolling or stationary on the court, that has come from elsewhere after the point started, a let should be called. See USTA Comment under Rule 20(g).*

Note to Rule 24: In a singles match, if, for the sake of convenience, a doubles Court is equipped with singles sticks for the purpose of a singles game, then the doubles posts and those portions of the net, cord or metal cable and the band outside such singles sticks shall at all times be permanent fixtures, and are not regarded as posts or parts of the net of a singles game.

A return that passes under the net cord between the singles stick and adjacent doubles post without touching either net cord, net or doubles post and falls within the area of play, is a good return. **USTA Comment:** *But in doubles this would be a "through" — loss of point.*

Case 1. A ball going out of Court hits a net post or singles stick and falls within the lines of the opponent's Court. Is the stroke good?

Decision. If a service: no, under Rule 10 *(c)*. If other than a service: yes, under Rule 24 *(a)*.

Case 2. Is it a good return if a player returns the ball holding his racket in both hands?

Decision. Yes.

Case 3. The service, or ball in play, strikes a ball lying in the Court. Is the point won or lost thereby? **USTA Comment:** *A ball that is touching a boundary line is considered to be "lying in the court".*

Decision. No. Play must continue. If it is not clear to the Umpire that the right ball is returned a let should be called.

Case 4. May a player use more than one racket at any time during play?

Decision. No; the whole implication of the Rules is singular.

Case 5. May a player request that a ball or balls lying in his opponent's Court be removed?

Decision. Yes, but not while a ball is in play. **USTA Comment:** *The request must be honored.*

RULE 25
Hindrance of a Player

In case a player is hindered in making a stroke by anything not within his control, except a permanent fixture of the Court, or except as provided for in Rule 21, a let shall be called.

Case 1. A spectator gets into the way of a player, who fails to return the ball. May the player then claim a let?

Decision. Yes, if in the Umpire's opinion he was obstructed by circumstances beyond his control, but not if due to permanent fixtures of the Court or the arrangements of the ground.

Case 2. A player is interfered with as in Case No. 1, and the Umpire calls a let. The Server had previously served a fault. Has he the right to two services?

Decision. Yes: as the ball is in play, the point, not merely the stroke, must be replayed as the Rule provides.

Case 3. May a player claim a let under Rule 25 because he thought his opponent was being hindered, and consequently did not expect the ball to be returned?

Decision. No.

Case 4. Is a stroke good when a ball in play hits another ball in the air?

Decision. A let should be called unless the other ball is in the air by the act of one of the players, in which case the Umpire will decide under Rule 21.

Case 5. If an Umpire or other judge erroneously calls "fault" or "out", and then corrects himself, which of the calls shall prevail?

Decision. A let must be called unless, in the opinion of the Umpire, neither player is hindered in his game, in which case the corrected call shall prevail.

Case 6. If the first ball served — a fault — rebounds, interfering with the Receiver at the time of the second service, may the Receiver claim a let?

Decision. Yes. But if he had an opportunity to remove the ball from the Court and negligently failed to do so, he may not claim a let.

Case 7. Is it a good stroke if the ball touches a stationary or moving object on the Court?

Decision. It is a good stroke unless the stationary object came into Court after the ball was put into play in which case a let must be called. If the ball in play strikes an object moving along or above the surface of the Court a let must be called.

Case 8. What is the ruling if the first service is a fault, the second service correct, and it becomes necessary to call a let either under the provision of Rule 25 or if the Umpire is unable to decide the point?

Decision. The fault shall be annulled and the whole point replayed.

USTA Comment: *See Rule 13 and Explanation thereto.*

RULE 26

Score in a Game

If a player wins his first point, the score is called 15 for that player; on winning his second point, the score is called 30 for that player; on winning his third point, the score is called 40 for that player, and the fourth point won by a player is scored game for that player except as below:

If both players have won three points, the score is called deuce; and the next point won by a player is scored advantage for that player. If the same player wins the next point, he wins the game; if the other player wins the next point the score is again called deuce; and so on, until a player wins the two points immediately following the score at deuce, when the game is scored for that player.

USTA Comment: *In matches played without an umpire the Server should announce, in a voice audible to his opponent and spectators, the set score at the beginning of each game, and (audible at least to his opponent) point scores as the game goes on. Misunderstandings will be avoided if this practice is followed.*

RULE 27

Score in a Set

(a) A player (or players) who first wins six games wins a set; except that he must win by a margin of two games over his opponent and where necessary a set is extended until this margin is achieved.

(b) The tie-break system of scoring may be adopted as an alternative to the advantage set system in paragraph (a) of this Rule provided the decision is announced in advance of the match.

USTA Comment: *See the Tie-Break System near the middle of this book.*

In this case, the following Rules shall be effective:

The tie-break shall operate when the score reaches six games all in any set except in the third or fifth set of a three set or five set match respectively when an ordinary advantage set shall be played, unless otherwise decided and announced in advance of the match.

The following system shall be used in a tie-break game.

Singles

(i) A player who first wins seven points shall win the game and the set provided he leads by a margin of two points. If the score reaches six points all the game shall be extended until this margin has been achieved. Numerical scoring shall be used throughout the tie-break game.

(ii) The player whose turn it is to serve shall be the server for the first point. His opponent shall be the server for the second and third points and thereafter each player shall serve alternately for two consecutive points until the winner of the game and set has been decided.

(iii) From the first point, each service shall be delivered alternately from the right and left courts, beginning from the right court. If service from a wrong half of the court occurs and is undetected, all play resulting from such wrong service or services shall stand, but the inaccuracy of station shall be corrected immediately it is discovered.

(iv) Players shall change ends after every six points and at the conclusion of the tie-break game.

(v) The tie-break game shall count as one game for the ball change, except that, if the balls are due to be changed at the beginning of the tie-break, the change shall be delayed until the second game of the following set.

Doubles

In doubles the procedure for singles shall apply. The player whose turn it is to serve shall be the server for the first point. Thereafter each player shall serve in rotation for two points, in the same order as previously in that set, until the winners of the game and set have been decided.

Rotation of Service

The player (or pair in the case of doubles) who served first in the tie-break game shall receive service in the first game of the following set.

Case 1. At six all the tie-break is played, although it has been decided and announced in advance of the match that an advantage set will be played. Are the points already played counted?

Decision. If the error is discovered before the ball is put in play for the second point, the first point shall count but the error shall be corrected immediately. If the error is discovered after the ball is put in play for the second point the game shall continue as a tie-break game.

Case 2. At six all, an advantage game is played, although it has been decided and announced in advance of the match that a tie-break will be played. Are the points already played counted?

Decision. If the error is discovered before the ball is put in play for the second point, the first point shall be counted but the error shall be corrected immediately. If the error is discovered after the ball is put in play for the second point an advantage set shall be continued. If the score thereafter reaches eight games all or a higher even number, a tie-break shall be played.

Case 3. If during the tie-break in a doubles game a partner receives out of turn, shall the order of receiving remain as altered until the end of the game?

Decision. If only one point has been played, the order of receiving shall be corrected immediately, and the point already played shall be counted. If the error is discovered after the ball is put in play for the second point, the order of receiving shall remain as altered.

Case 4. If during a tie-break in a singles or doubles game, a player serves out of turn, shall the order of service remain as altered until the end of the game?

Decision. If only one point has been played, the order of service shall be corrected immediately and the point already played shall be counted. If the error is discovered after the ball is put in play for the second point, the order of service shall remain as altered.

RULE 28

Maximum Number of Sets

The maximum number of sets in a match shall be 5, or, where women take part, 3.

RULE 29

Role of Court Officials

In matches where an Umpire is appointed, his decision shall be final; but where a Referee is appointed, an appeal shall lie to him from the decision of an Umpire on a question of law, and in all such cases the decision of the Referee shall be final.

In matches where assistants to the Umpire are appointed (Linesmen, Net-cord Judges, Foot-fault Judges) their decisions shall be final on questions of fact except that if in the opinion of an Umpire a clear mistake has been made he shall have the right to change the decision of an assistant or order a let to be played. When such an assistant is unable to give a decision he shall indicate this immediately to the Umpire who shall give a decision. When an Umpire is unable to give a decision on a question of fact he shall order a let to be played.

In Davis Cup matches or other team competitions where a Referee is on Court, any decision can be changed by the Referee, who may also instruct an Umpire to order a let to be played.

The Referee, in his discretion, may at any time postpone a match on account of darkness or the condition of the ground or the weather. In any case of postponement the previous score and previous occupancy of Courts shall hold good, unless the Referee and the players unanimously agree otherwise.

Case 1. The Umpire orders a let, but a player claims that the point should not be replayed. May the Referee be requested to give a decision?

Decision. Yes. A question of tennis law, that is an issue relating to the application of specific facts, shall first be determined by the Umpire. However, if the Umpire is uncertain or if a player appeals from his determination, then the Referee shall be requested to give a decision, and his decision is final.

Case 2. A ball is called out, but a player claims that the ball was good. May the Referee give a ruling?

Decision. No. This is a question of fact, that is an issue relating to what actually occurred during a specific incident, and the decision of the on-court officials is therefore final.

Case 3. May an Umpire overrule a Linesman at the end of a rally if, in his opinion, a clear mistake has been made during the course of a rally?

Decision. No, unless in his opinion the opponent was hindered. Otherwise an Umpire may only overrule a Linesman if he does so immediately after the mistake has been made.

USTA Comment: *See Rule 17, Case 1.*

Case 4. A Linesman calls a ball out. The Umpire was unable to see clearly, although he thought the ball was in. May he overrule the Linesman?

Decision. No. An Umpire may only overrule if he considers that a call was incorrect beyond all reasonable doubt. He may only overrule a ball determined good by a Linesman if he has been able to see a space between the ball and the line; and he may only overrule a ball determined out, or a fault, by a Linesman if he has seen the ball hit the line, or fall inside the line.

Case 5. May a Linesman change his call after the Umpire has given the score?

Decision. Yes. If a Linesman realises he has made an error, he may make a correction provided he does so immediately.

Case 6. A player claims his return shot was good after a Linesman called "out". May the Umpire overrule the Linesman?

Decision. No. An Umpire may never overrule as a result of a protest or an appeal by a player.

RULE 30
Continuous Play and Rest Periods

Play shall be continuous from the first service until the match is concluded, in accordance with the following provisions:

(a) If the first service is a fault, the second service must be struck by the Server without delay.

The Receiver must play to the reasonable pace of the Server and must be ready to receive when the Server is ready to serve.

When changing ends a maximum of one minute thirty seconds shall elapse from the moment the ball goes out of play at the end of the game to the time the ball is struck for the first point of the next game.

The Umpire shall use his discretion when there is interference which makes it impractical for play to be continuous.

The organisers of international circuits and team events recognised by the ITF may determine the time allowed between points, which shall not at any time exceed 30 seconds.

(b) Play shall never be suspended, delayed or interfered with for the purpose of enabling a player to recover his strength, breath, or physical condition.

However, in the case of accidental injury, the Umpire may allow a one-time three minute suspension for that injury.

The organisers of international circuits and team events recognised by the ITF may extend the one-time suspension period from three minutes to five minutes.

USTA Comment: *There is an important distinction between loss of condition caused by an accident during the match and natural loss of condition attributable to fatigue, illness or exertion (example: cramps, muscle pull, vertigo, strained back). Accidental loss embodies a sprained ankle or actual injury from such mishaps as collision with a net post or net, a cut from a fall, contact with a chair or backstop, or being hit with a ball, racket, or other object.*

An injured player shall not be permitted to leave the playing area. If, in the opinion of the Umpire, there is a genuine toilet emergency, a bona fide toilet visit by a player is permissible and is not to be considered natural loss of condition. A doctor or trainer may treat a player during an accidental injury suspension or during any 90-second changeover upon the approval of the Chair Umpire or the Referee.

(c) If, through circumstances outside the control of the player, his clothing, footwear or equipment (excluding racket) becomes out of adjustment in such a way that it is impossible or undesirable for him to play on, the Umpire may suspend play while the maladjustment is rectified.

(d) The Umpire may suspend or delay play at any time as may be necessary and appropriate.

USTA Comment: *When a match is resumed after an interruption of more than ten minutes necessitated by abnormal weather or other conditions, it is permissible for the players to engage in a re-warm-up that may be of the same duration as that at the start of the match; it may be done using the balls that were in play at the time of the interruption, and the time for the next ball change shall not be affected by this. There shall be no re-warm-up after an authorized intermission or after an interruption of ten minutes or less.*

(e) After the third set, or when women take part the second set, either player is entitled to a rest, which shall not exceed 10 minutes, or in countries situated between latitude 15 degrees north and lati-

tude 15 degrees south, 45 minutes and furthermore, when necessitated by circumstances not within the control of the players, the Umpire may suspend play for such a period as he may consider necessary. If play is suspended and is not resumed until a later day the rest may be taken only after the third set (or when women take part the second set) of play on such a later day, completion of an unfinished set being counted as one set.

If play is suspended and is not resumed until 10 minutes have elapsed in the same day the rest may be taken only after three consecutive sets have been played without interruption (or when women take part two sets), completion of an unfinished set being counted as one set.

Any nation and/or committee organising a tournament, match or competition, other than the International Tennis Championships (Davis Cup and Federation Cup), is at liberty to modify this provision or omit it from its regulations provided this is announced before the event commences.

USTA Rules Regarding Rest Periods

Regular MEN's and WOMEN's, and MEN's and WOMEN's Amateur — Paragraph (e) of Rule 30 applies, except that a tournament using tie-breaks may eliminate rest periods provided advance notice is given.

BOYS' 18 — All matches in this division shall be best of three sets with NO REST PERIOD, except that in interscholastic, state, sectional and national championships the FINAL ROUND may be best-of-five sets. If such a final requires more than three sets to decide it, a rest of 10 minutes after the third set is mandatory. Special Note: In severe temperature-humidity conditions the Referee may rule that a 10-minute rest may be taken in a Boys' 18 best-of-three before the third set. However, to be valid this must be done before the match is started, and as a matter of the Referee's independent judgment.

BOYS' 16, 14 and 12, and GIRLS' 18, 16, 14 and 12 — All matches in these categories shall be best of three sets. A 10-minute rest before the third set is MANDATORY in Girls' 12, 14 and 16, and BOYS' 12 and 14. The rest period is OPTIONAL in GIRLS' 18 and BOYS' 16. (Optional means at the option of any competitor).

All SENIOR divisions (35 and over), Mother-Daughter, Father-Son and similar combinations: Under conventional scoring, all matches best of three sets, with rest period at any player's option.

When 'NO-AD' scoring is used in a tournament the committee may stipulate that there will be no rest periods. Two conditions of this stipulation are: (1) Advance notice must be given on entry blanks for the event, and (2) The Referee is empowered to reinstate the normal rest periods for matches played under unusually severe temperature-humidity conditions; to be valid, such reinstatement must be announced before a given match or series of matches is started, and be a matter of the Referee's independent judgment.

USTA Comment: *When a player competes in an event designated for players of a bracket whose rules as to intermissions, length of match, number of matches per day, etc., are geared to a different physical status, the player cannot ask for allowances based on age or sex. For example, a 55-year old player competing in a Senior 45 national championship may not refuse to play two singles matches in one day, which he could legally refuse to do in a Senior 55 national championship.*

(f) A tournament committee has the discretion to decide the time allowed for a warm-up period prior to a match but this may not exceed five minutes and must be announced before the event commences.

(g) When approved point penalty and non-accumulative point penalty systems are in operation, the Umpire shall make his decisions within the terms of those systems.

(h) Upon violation of the principle that play shall be continuous the Umpire may, after giving due warning, disqualify the offender.

RULE 31
Coaching

During the playing of a match in a team competition, a player may receive coaching from a captain who is sitting on the court only when he changes ends at the end of a game, but not when he changes ends during a tie-break game.

A player may not receive coaching during the playing of any other match.

After due warning an offending player may be disqualified. When an approved point penalty system is in operation, the Umpire shall impose penalties according to that system.

Case 1. Should a warning be given, or the player be disqualified, if the coaching is given by signals in an unobtrusive manner?

Decision. The Umpire must take action as soon as he becomes aware that coaching is being given verbally or by signals. If the Umpire is unaware that coaching is being given, a player may draw his attention to the fact that advice is being given.

Case 2. Can a player receive coaching during the ten minute rest in a five set match, or when play is interrupted and he leaves the court?

Decision. Yes. In these circumstances, when the player is not on the court, there is no restriction on coaching.

Note: The word "coaching" includes any advice or instruction.

RULE 32
Changing Balls

In cases where balls are to be changed after a specified number of games, if the balls are not changed in the correct sequence, the mistake shall be corrected when the player, or pair in the case of doubles, who should have served with new balls is next due to serve. Thereafter the balls shall be changed so that the number of games between changes shall be that originally agreed.

The Doubles Game

RULE 33

The above Rules shall apply to the Doubles Game except as below.

RULE 34
The Doubles Court

For the Doubles Game, the Court shall be 36 feet (10.97m.) in width, i.e. 4½ feet (1.37m.) wider on each side than the Court for the Singles Game, and those portions of the singles side-lines which lie between the two service-lines shall be called the service side-lines. In other respects, the Court shall be similar to that described in Rule 1, but the portions of the singles side-lines between the base-line and service-line on each side of the net may be omitted if desired.

USTA Case 1. In doubles the Server claims the right to stand at the corner of the court as marked by the doubles sideline. Is the foregoing correct or is it necessary that the Server stand within the limits of the center mark and the singles sideline?

Decision. The Server has the right to stand anywhere back of the baseline between the center mark extension and the doubles sideline extension.

RULE 35
Order of Service in Doubles

The order of serving shall be decided at the beginning of each set as follows:

The pair who have to serve in the first game of each set shall decide which partner shall do so and the opposing pair shall decide similarly for the second game. The partner of the player who served in the first game shall serve in the third; the partner of the player who served in the second game shall serve in the fourth, and so on in the same order in all the subsequent games of a set.

Case 1. In doubles, one player does not appear in time to play, and his partner claims to be allowed to play single-handed against the opposing players. May he do so?

Decision. No.

RULE 36
Order of Receiving in Doubles

The order of receiving the service shall be decided at the beginning of each set as follows:

The pair who have to receive the service in the first game shall decide which partner shall receive the first service, and that partner shall continue to receive the first service in every odd game throughout that set. The opposing pair shall likewise decide which partner shall receive the first service in the second game and that partner shall continue to receive the first service in every even game throughout that set. Partners shall receive the service alternately throughout each game.

Case 1. Is it allowable in doubles for the Server's partner or the Receiver's partner to stand in a position that obstructs the view of the Receiver?

Decision. Yes. The Server's partner or the Receiver's partner may take any position on his side of the net in or out of the Court that he wishes.

RULE 37
Service Out of Turn in Doubles

If a partner serves out of his turn, the partner who ought to have served shall serve as soon as the mistake is discovered, but all points scored, and any faults served before such discovery, shall be reckoned. If a game shall have been completed before such discovery, the order of service remains as altered.

USTA Comment: *For an exception to Rule 37 see Case 4 under Rule 27.*

RULE 38
Error in Order of Receiving in Doubles

If during a game the order of receiving the service is changed by the Receivers it shall remain as altered until the end of the game in which the mistake is discovered, but the partners shall resume their original order of receiving in the next game of that set in which they are Receivers of the service.

USTA Comment: *For an exception to Rule 38 see Case 3 under Rule 27.*

RULE 39
Service Fault in Doubles

The service is a fault as provided for by Rule 10, or if the ball touches the Server's partner or anything which he wears or carries; but if the ball served touches the partner of the Receiver, or anything which he wears or carries, not being a let under Rule 14(a) before it hits the ground, the Server wins the point.

RULE 40
Playing the Ball in Doubles

The ball shall be struck alternately by one or other player of the opposing pairs, and if a player touches the ball in play with his racket in contravention of this Rule, his opponents win the point.

USTA Comment: *This means that, in the course of making one return, only one member of a doubles team may hit the ball. If both of them hit the ball, either simultaneously or consecutively, it is an illegal return. The partners themselves do not have to "alternate" in making returns. Mere clashing of rackets does not make a return illegal, if it is clear that only one racket touched the ball.*

THE TIE-BREAK SYSTEM

A tournament committee must announce before the start of its tournament the details concerning its use of tie-breaks. A tournament that has been authorized by the USTA or by a USTA Section to use VASSS No-Ad scoring may use the 9-point tie-break in any set played under No-Ad; it may change to the 12-point tie-break in its later rounds. No-Ad scoring is authorized for tournaments held at the Sectional Championship level and below, and for consolation matches in any tournament (excluding any USTA National Junior Championship). Other than the foregoing exceptions, all sanctioned tournaments using tie-breaks will use only the 12-point tie-break. Rule 27 establishes the procedure for the 12-point tie-break game. For a more detailed explanation see below.

If a ball change is due on a tie-break game it will be deferred until the second game of the next set. A tie-break game counts as one game in reckoning ball changes. The score of the tie-break set will be written 7-6 (x) or 6-7 (x), with the score of the winner of the match entered first, followed by the score of the tie-break game in parentheses, such as (10-8) or (8-10), with the score of the winner of the match again entered first. Changes of ends during a tie-break game are to be made within the normal time allowed between points.

The 12-Point Tie-Break

Singles: A, having served the first game of the set, serves the first point from the right court; B serves points 2 and 3 (left and right), A serves points 4 and 5 (left and right); B serves point 6 (left) and after they change ends, point 7 (right); A serves points 8 and 9 (left and right); B serves points 10 and 11 (left and right), and A serves point 12 (left). A player who reaches 7 points during these first 12 points wins the game and set. If the score has reached 6 points all, the players change ends and continue in the same pattern until one player establishes a margin of two points, which gives him the game and set. Note that the players change ends every six points, and that the player who serves the last point of one of these 6-point segments also serves the first point of the next one (from right court). For a following set the players change ends, and B serves the first game.

Doubles follows the same pattern, with partners preserving their serving sequence. Assuming A-B versus C-D, with A having served the first game of the set: A serves the first point (right); C serves points 2 and 3 (left and right); B serves points 4 and 5 (left and right); D serves point 6 (left) and the teams change ends. D serves point 7 (right); A serves points 8 and 9 (left and right); C serves points 10 and 11 (left and right); B serves point 12 (left). A team that wins 7 points during these first 12 points wins the game and set. If the score has reached 6 points all, the teams change ends. B then serves point 13, (right) and they continue until one team establishes a two-point margin and thus wins the game and set. As in singles, they change ends for one game to start a following set, with team C-D to serve first.

The 9-Point Tie-Break

Singles: With A having served the first game of the set, he serves points 1 and 2, right court and left; then B serves points 3 and 4, right and left. Players change ends. A serves points 5 and 6, right and left, and B serves points 7 and 8, right and left. If the score reaches 4

points all B serves point 9, right or left at the election of A. The first player to win 5 points wins the game and set. The players stay for one game to start the next set, and B is the first server.

Doubles: The same format as in singles applies, with each player serving from the same end of the court in the tie-break game that he served from during the set. (Note that this operates to alter the sequence of serving by the partners on the *second*-serving team. With A-B versus C-D, if the serving sequence during the set was A-C-B-D the sequence becomes A-D-B-C in the tie-break.)

VASSS NO AD SCORING

The No-Ad procedure is simply what the name implies: the first player to win four points wins the game, the 7th point of a game becoming a game point for each player. The receiver has the choice of advantage court or deuce court to which the service is to be delivered on the 7th point. If a No-Ad set reaches 6-games all a tie-break shall be used, which is normally the 9-point tie-break.

Note: The score-calling may be either in the conventional terms or in simple numbers, i.e., "zero, one, two, three, game" at the option of the tournament management.

Cautionary Note

Any ITF-sponsored tournament should get special authorization from ITF before using No-Ad.

If you have a rules problem, send full details, enclosing a stamped self-addressed envelope, to Nick Powel, USTA Tennis Rules Committee, 3147 South 14th Street, Arlington, Virginia, 22204, and you will be sent a prompt explanation.